My Little Golden Book About

RUTH BADER GINSBURG

By Shana Corey

Illustrated by Margeaux Lucas

The editors would like to thank Lisa Kathleen Graddy, Curator, Division of Political History, National Museum of American History, for her assistance in the preparation of this book.

A GOLDEN BOOK • NEW YORK

Text copyright © 2021 by Shana Corey
Cover art and interior illustrations copyright © 2021 by Margeaux Lucas
All rights reserved. Published in the United States by Golden Books, an imprint of Random House Children's Books, a division of Penguin Random House LLC, 1745 Broadway, New York, NY 10019. Golden Books, A Golden Book, A Little Golden Book, the G colophon, and the distinctive gold spine are registered trademarks of Penguin Random House LLC.
rhcbooks.com
Educators and librarians, for a variety of teaching tools, visit us at RHTeachersLibrarians.com
Library of Congress Control Number: 2019946272
ISBN 978-0-593-17280-3 (trade) — ISBN 978-0-593-17281-0 (ebook)
Printed in the United States of America
10 9 8 7 6 5 4 3 2

RUTH BADER GINSBURG WAS A SUPREME COURT JUSTICE AND A HERO IN THE FIGHT FOR WOMEN'S RIGHTS.

Ruth Bader was born in Brooklyn, New York, in 1933. Her neighborhood was filled with people of many different backgrounds—Irish and Italian, Polish and Russian, Catholic, and Jewish, like Ruth.

Ruth roller-skated and rode bikes and jumped rope. She went to school and took piano lessons and went to summer camp. She loved opera. And she loved to read. Ruth's mother took her to the library every Friday. Ruth liked to read about women and girls who had adventures and did things. Ruth wanted to do things, too.

"READING SHAPED MY DREAMS.
AND MORE READING HELPED ME
MAKE MY DREAMS COME TRUE."

But not everyone in the United States had the opportunity to do the things they wanted. People were often treated differently because of the color of their skin or their religion. Boys and girls were also treated differently. Families sometimes sent their sons to college, but not their daughters.

In Ruth's school, girls had to learn to cook and sew while the boys were taught to build things. Ruth wished she could learn what the boys learned. When she grew up, Ruth would work to make things more equal for girls and boys.

Ruth's parents hadn't gone to college, but her mother encouraged her to get a good education. Ruth's mom wanted her to grow up to be independent. She taught Ruth to stand up for her beliefs—but not to waste time being angry.

Ruth worked hard and got good grades.
When she graduated from high school, she
won a scholarship to Cornell University.
The other students were impressed with
how smart Ruth was. One of those students
was a young man named Marty Ginsburg.

Marty and Ruth fell in love. After they graduated, they got married and had a baby girl. They named her Jane.

Ruth believed lawyers could help people by making sure the laws treated everyone fairly. So she decided to go to law school. It was tough with a new baby, but Ruth was determined. She managed to be one of the top students!

Even so, no one would hire her. Some law firms didn't want to hire Jewish people. Others didn't want to hire women. Ruth never forgot this. She spent her career fighting to make discrimination of all kinds illegal.

Ruth decided to become a law professor. There were very few law professors in the United States who were women, but that didn't stop her.

Ruth also cofounded the Women's Rights Project to fight for women's equality under the law. And Ruth and Marty welcomed a new baby, James, to their family.

For the next several years, Ruth argued case after case to help expand women's equality. Some of the cases were presented to the highest court in the United States—the Supreme Court.

"REAL CHANGE . . . HAPPENS ONE STEP AT A TIME."

Ruth argued that men and women should be treated the same by their employers, by the government, and by the law. And with each case that she won, the law moved one step closer to treating everyone equally.

Ruth spent decades—in law school, as a professor, and with the cases she argued— paving the way for women. She was known to be hardworking and fair. In 1980, Ruth became a judge in Washington, D.C. And in 1993, President Bill Clinton nominated Ruth to the United States Supreme Court.

Ruth became the second woman and the first Jewish woman in history to be a U.S. Supreme Court Justice.

There are nine Justices on the Supreme Court. After lawyers present their arguments in a case, the Justices take a vote. Sometimes most of the Justices agreed with Ruth. But sometimes they didn't agree with her and the Supreme Court ruled in a way that she thought was wrong.

When that happened, Ruth remembered her mother's lessons. Instead of getting angry, she stood up for her beliefs and wrote a dissent— a disagreement. Dissents don't usually change the ruling, but they help show people why it might have been wrong. Lawmakers might read it and create new laws. And future judges might learn from it and one day rule a case differently.

Ruth Bader Ginsburg is a hero in the fight for equality. She spent her life making the United States more equal for everyone. She paved the way, and now we can all help take the next steps. We can stand up for what we believe in and fight to make the United States fairer for all—

JUST LiKe RUTH.